Trump Trial Circus: Davidson and Hope

Info Broker and Press Secretary Testify Against Trump

by Matthew Russell Lee

Inner City Press

April 30-May 2, 2024

TABLE OF CONTENTS

I. Trump Trial, April 30, 2024

When the Trump trial resumed on April 30, the prosecution's main witness after Pecker was his negotiation partner Keith Davidson.

 He described himself a lawyer with media clients, and said these include reality TV clients. And porn stars?

 In reading for the jury his text messages with Pecker's editor Dylan Howard, Davidson came across his line about Karen McDougal being under pressure from what Davidson called the "estrogen mafia."

   This turned off many of the prosecution's fans online - and perhaps some of the jurors.

Could it be even more so with Michael Cohen? And how would Team Trump cross-examine Davidson?

Todd Blanche's attempted cross examination of banker Farro led nowhere, but one wondered why it was Flagstar Bank, his current employer, who was paying for his lawyer for testimony on what he did and didn't do while at First Republic, given to Chase. It was reported as if a scoop that the Trump lawyers would be crossing more aggressively. But of course, after kids gloves with Trump's assistant Rhona Graff. The transcript of Friday included Trump asking "Are you alright?" with no answer. There will be answers.

Song of Davidson I

When I saw Los Angeles lawyer
I mean extortionist
My trade is celebrity scandal
I take forty-five percent

On Karen I hit paydirt
On Stormy? Not so much.
I said, Let Gina take it
But came back for ten large.

Making Donald Trump's code name
My old hockey buddy
Was the icing on the cake
I finally got to brag about it
Under immunity.
So life is good
Did I say, LA lawyer?

Trump

"One weekday One airplane Two states
So which shall they be?
There was rain in Carolina
So indoor in Wisconsin
I'll be back for the convention.

Eight percent TelePrompTer I told 'em
But which eight percent?
I can trash Merchan, Bragg and the Big Guy
Not the daughter, the jurors
Nor E. Jean if I don't want to pay more
And I don't.

A president can pardon
But how pay those judgments?
I could post a bond
But could I float or issue one?
Question for another day

November 5, that'd be
If we get there."

The trial day, April 30, 2024

[Trump has arrived, blue suit, red tie. Pool photos taken. Then Trump leans right and whispers in Todd Blanche's ear]

All rise!

Justice Merchan: Mr. Blanche, which days had you requested for the high school graduation?

Blanche: May 17 and June 3

Justice Merchan: We finished jury selection quickly, so I think Mr. Trump can attend the graduation on May 17. June 3, not if the jury is deliberating... I will now rule on contempt. On the ten incidents, the people have met their burden on all but incident 1

Justice Merchan: Mr. Trump is fined $1000 for each: 2-3, and 4-10. Please bring in the witness, then the jury.
[Jury enters]

[Note: the written order, screenshot below, says that the nine posts at issue are to be taken down by 2:15 pm today]

Justice Merchan [to Farro] Welcome. People?

Prosecutor: Let's focus on this First Republic document. What is it?

Farro: It's a signature card for Essential Consultants LLC.

Prosecutor: Who are the signers?
Farro: Only Michael Cohen.

Prosecutor: What are these documents?
Farro: Tax ID number provided by the IRS.
Prosecutor: Where was the LLC formed?
Farro: Delaware. Most LLCs I deal with are formed there.
Prosecutor: And this EIN, what is it?
Farro: Like a Social Security number for a business

Prosecutor: Why did it take hours to open the account?

Farro: Michael Cohen is not our only customer. There are other things that take precedence.

Prosecutor: Did Mr. Cohen said it would be used to make a contribution on behalf of a political candidate?

Farro: No

Prosecutor: Did any of the opening paperwork indicate the account would be used to pay an adult film star?

Farro: No. That is an industry we do not work with.

Prosecutor: What's this?

Farro: Transfer from home equity line of credit to Essential Consultants LLC

Prosecutor: And on this document, who is Laura Cohen?

Farro: Michael Cohen's spouse.

Prosecutor: How many people had to approve this?
Farro: Two.
Prosecutor: What's this?
Farro: A wire authorization form, from Essential Consultants

Prosecutor: What is the listed purpose?
Farro: Retainer. That's what Michael Cohen told us.
Prosecutor: What's this?
Farro: An outgoing wire transfer form, an internal document.
Prosecutor: People's 378, what is it?
Farro: Email to Michael Cohen that wire's on way

Prosecutor: Who was it wired to?
Farro: Keith Davidson and Associates.
Prosecutor: Did any of this say it was on behalf of a political candidate?
Farro: No.
Prosecutor: No further questions.

Justice Merchan: Any cross?

Trump's lawyer Blanche: Good morning

Trump's lawyer Blanche: Before today, you met with the People?

Farro: Please explain what the People means.
Blanche: The prosecutors. Did you meet them last year?
Farro: Yes. Once. And twice this year.
Blanche: Did you meet other law enforcement?
Farro: Yes, in DC

Trump's lawyer Blanche: When did you do to DC?
Farro: In 2018.
Blanche: Who's paying for your lawyer today?
Farro: Flagstar, my employer.
Blanche: Not Chase?
Farro: No, Flagstar.
Blanche: You opened Michael Cohen's account?
Farro: I don't do the paperwork

Trump's lawyer Blanche: You said Mr. Cohen was difficult?
Farro: Yes... His desire that everything be done quickly. I try to rationalize with clients that things may not be so urgent.
Blanche: As of March 23, 2023, was Cohen still your client?
Farro: No.

Farro: Once this information came out, I was taken away from the relationship [with Michael Cohen]
Trump's lawyer Blanche: Are you familiar with the term "de-risking"?

Farro: I'm not familiar with that term.
Blanche: If the bank no longer wants a customer...

Trump's lawyer Blanche: You had no reason to think Mr. Cohen was opening up a shell corporation. If he had told you?
Farro: I would not have opened it. Unless it was to own a home or yacht or jet, to keep ownership confidential.

Trump's lawyer Blanche: Do you remember getting an email bounce-back on March 17, 2017 telling you Michel Cohen was now President Trump's personal lawyer?
Farro: Yes, but that was an errant email.
Blanche: What's a PEP?
Farro: Politically exposed person

Trump's lawyer Blanche: Are you aware that an official's lawyer is also considered a PEP?
Farro: I was not aware of that.
Blanche: And if he had been identified as a PEP-
Prosecutor: Objection!

Trump's lawyer Blanche: Let me ask this way - if you have ever had a PEP, what does it entail?
Farro: We monitor them.
Blanche: In September 2017, did Michael Cohen

say he needed to speak with you?
Farro: I do not remember.

Trump's lawyer Blanche: You never spoke with Michael Cohen about Donald Trump?
Farro: No.
Blanche: And you never spoke with President Trump?
Farro: No.
Blanche: No further questions.

Justice Merchan: Re-direct?

Prosecutor: Why was Michael Cohen cut off?
Farro: Not telling the truth.
Prosecutor: No further questions.
Re-cross
Trump's lawyer Blanche: Did the shut down mean that appropriate due diligence wasn't done in the first place?
Farro: Not necessarily.
No further Qs

Justice Merchan: Jurors, let's take our morning recess.
[Jurors leave]

Prosecutor: I'm handing up agreed redactions. The

red ones are those still in dispute. In this one, in the midst of the negotiations around Stormy Daniels, Ms. Rodriguez says "shady sh*t"

Prosecutor: In this one, it says "Daily Mail is afraid of Trump." Ms. Rodriguez is not alleged to be a co-conspirator, unlike Dylan Howard, so there are not coming in for the truth of the matter asserted. Of these three, we can live without the first

Trump's lawyer Blanche: These could confuse the jury, "shady sh*t," even with a limiting instruction. "The Daily Mail is scared of Trump," that's hearsay. That's our very strong belief.

Justice Merchan: I'll rule after the break. Anything else?

Prosecutor II: With today's finding of contempt, we would intend to cross examine the defendant if he chooses to testify. We are ready for a Sandoval hearing
Trump's lawyer Blanche: We haven't even read it yet.
Justice Merchan: Read it, and then respond

Prosecutor II: We should be able to elicit evidence about the defendant's harassment online of Michael

Cohen and Stormy Daniels, in light of the opening statements.

Trump's lawyer Blanche: There should be a proffer. We will cross examine about bias, sure

Prosecutor II: It shows consciousness of guilt.

Trump's lawyer Blanche: President Trump was speaking about Cohen's plea in SDNY, where President Trump was never charged.
Justice Merchan: Do you need a ruling on that?
Prosecutor II: By Thursday would help us.

Justice Merchan: See you in a few minutes.

[They've back]
Justice Merchan: The defense opened the door, I think they have, but what can be it be used for? You can use it to rebut, for example that they are not making as much money as people think.
Prosecutor: So People's 171 is in, with redactions.

Justice Merchan: A juror wants to know if they can fly on May 24, before Memorial Day. Do the parties agree?

They do.
[Jury enters]

Justice Merchan: We will not be working May 17, nor May 24.

Prosecutor: People call Dr. Robert X. Browning

Prosecutor: What is your job?
Browning: I am archivist at C-SPAN.
Prosecutor: Was C-SPAN subpoenaed by DANY?
Browning: Yes. We turned videos over.
Prosecutor: Can you recognize Donald Trump?
Browning: Yes.
Prosecutor: Do you have the NC rally in October 2016?
Yes

Prosecutor: We offer into evidence. Let's play it.
[Trump on screen: It's a phony deal... I have no idea who these women are... They get some free fame...]
Prosecutor: Dr. Browning, is that a portion?
Browning: Yes it is.

Prosecutor: Next exhibit.
[Trump in front of a Trump Pence sign, "these are all lies" Then, in front of flags, Trump speaks on

Michael Cohen.]
Prosecutor: No further questions.
Justice Merchan: Your witness.
Trump's lawyer Blanche: We have no questions.

Prosecutor: The People call Phillip Thompson
[Esquire Deposition Solutions, LLC]
Prosecutor: You are a records custodian?
Thompson: Yes. Under subpoena.
Prosecutor: Did you turn over the transcript and
video of an Oct 22 deposition in Carroll v. Trump
Yes

Prosecutor: It was October 2022 - please play is
[Note: Inner City Press filed in Carroll v. Trump
case to get this video released to the public and it
was - we put in on YouTube here:

Prosecutor: please read the transcript
Thompson: Ms. Kaplan: Are you familiar with the
Access Hollywood tape. Answer: Yes
Prosecutor: No further questions.
Trump's lawyer Blanche: We don't have any
questions.
Justice Merchan: You may step down.

Prosecutor: The People call Keith Davidson.. How
old are you?

Davidson: 53. I graduated from Boston College and Whittier Law School. Davidson and Associates, we do media cases

Prosecutor: Any sexual abuse cases?

Davidson: Yes.

Prosecutor: In 2015 to 2017 did you use non-disclosure agreements?
Davidson: Yes.

Prosecutor: Do you know Gina Rodriguez?
Davidson: Yes. She manages reality TV type talent.

Prosecutor: Have you represented Gina Davidson?
A: Gina *Rodriguez*
Prosecutor: Sorry

Prosecutor: How about Dylan Howard?
Davidson: A friend. Sometimes we worked together, overlaps about tabloid media.
Prosecutor: Did you negotiate the sale of certain stories to tabloids?
Davidson: Rarely.

Prosecutor: Are you familiar with David Pecker?

Davidson: Yes. AMI and the National Enquirer, Dylan Howard's boss. I've only dealt with him about four times in my life

Prosecutor: And Michael Cohen?
Davidson: Yes, about my client Ms. Clifford, also known as Stormy Daniels.

Prosecutor: Do you recognize this thumb drive?
Davidson: Yes. I produced these records pursuant to a subpoena.

Prosecutor: Do you know Karen McDougal?

Davidson: Yes. I met her 25 years ago. She was dating a friend of mine. Then I represented her about a personal interaction she had.
Prosecutor: With who(m)?

Davidson: Donald Trump. Her brother-in-law linked us

Prosecutor: Look at your retainer. What does this mean?

Davidson: There were exclusive arrangements with media outlets, in exchange for money.

Prosecutor: Did you inform Ms. McDougal that you could negotiate for her?

Davidson: I won't discuss our communications

Prosecutor: Let's look at your text messages with Dylan Howard. Expand them. What did this mean?

Davidson: That he would get more for this story than anyone. David Pecker published Trump Magazine AMI had implied they had endorsed Mr. Trump's candidacy

Prosecutor: Did you arrange a meeting between Ms. McDougal and Dylan Howard?

Davidson: Yes. Johnny Crawford was also there. He's a friend of Karen's, a police officer from Arizona. We discussed the personal interaction of Ms. McDougal with Donald Trump

Prosecutor: Since this was in front of others, what did Ms. McDougal say?

Davidson: That she had a romantic affair of several weeks or months with Donald Trump some years ago.

Prosecutor: What was the purpose of meeting?

Davidson: It was sort of a proffer session

Davidson: Dylan said he would go back to New York and run it up the flagpole.
Prosecutor: Who?

Davidson: Pecker. But they did not buy it right away. They said Karen McDougal did not have enough documentary evidence

Davidson: I said, "Don't forget Michael Cohen... The girl is being cornered by the estrogen mafia"

Prosecutor: What did you mean?

Davidson: It was a regrettable text I sent. There were several women leaning on Karen to sign the deal with ABC
Prosecutor: How did Dylan Howard reply?

Davidson: That they would have an offer for us by Monday. They he said, Get me an offer, all in, perhaps a fitness component. She wanted to rejuvenate her career. She wanted to avoid the scarlet letter, being the other woman

Davidson: Then Dylan said, We are going to lay it on thick for her. Karen was teetering between National Enquirer versus ABC. I said, "Throw in an ambassadorship for me. I'm thinking, the Isle of Man." It was sort of a jest.
Prosecutor: Why was that funny?

Davidson: Well, I don't think that the Isle of Man is even a country. So no ambassador there. It was a reference to Donald Trump, that if this help him and he won, there would be jobs
Prosecutor: What did Dylan Howard write?
Davidson: She'll get more than from ABC

Justice Merchan: Let's take out lunch break.
[Jurors leave]

[They've back]

Justice Merchan: Let's get the witness, please
[Keith Davidson returns. Jury enters]

Prosecutor: Good afternoon Mr. Howard! Oh, sorry, Davidson. Please look at these texts.

Davidson: Dylan wanted the deal between Karen McDougal and AMI to happen.

Davidson: Dylan wrote, "F- it, not my money, I'll just ask."

Prosecutor: Is the full F word written out in the text?

Davidson: Yes. Then he wrote, She's getting pressed by Ronda Schwartz.

Prosecutor: Who's she?

Davidson: She worked for Brian Ross of ABC

Davidson: Then AMI's general counsel set me a contract that didn't jibe with what had been negotiated with Dylan. I replied, Need to handle this quickly. The general counsel wanted to call Michael Cohen.

Prosecutor: Did you ask why?

Davidson: I don't remember

Davidson: I had dealt with Michael Cohen in 2011 and had not enjoyed it. So I was trying to avoid it.

Prosecutor: Did Dylan say anything else?

Davidson: F*cking Jesus.
Prosecutor: It's okay, you're just quoting. Did you call Cohen?
Davidson: Yes

Davidson: After the deal closed with AMI I called Michael Cohen, as a professional courtesy, about a deal involving his client.

Prosecutor: What client?

Davidson: Donald Trump

Prosecutor: Was he a named party?

Davidson: No. But it benefited him. Cohen was pleased

Prosecutor: Based on non-privileged communications to which you were privy, what married man benefited from this?

Davidson: Donald Trump.

Prosecutor: How much went to you?

Davidson: 45%

Prosecutor: Did you think AMI would ever publish it?

Davidson: No.

Prosecutor: Why?

Davidson: It was said AMI would not want to hurt Karen's brand. But mostly, there was an affinity between David Pecker and Donald Trump - so, to not hurt Trump

Prosecutor: You mean his campaign?
Davidson: Yes.

Prosecutor: Had ABC offered a role on Dancing with the Starts?

Davidson: "Best efforts" were discussed.

Prosecutor: Do you know Stormy Daniels?
Davidson: Yes. She was a client of mine, managed by Gina Rodriguez. I spoke with them in 2011 about TheDirty dot com

Prosecutor: What was it about?

Davidson: A blog post that Stormy Daniels and Donald Trump had had an intimate interaction. Gina told me some jerk had called and threatened to sue.

Prosecutor: Who was that jerk?
Davidson: Donald Trump

Prosecutor: What was his accusation?
Davidson: I don't know. He was just screaming and

threatening to sue. So I sent a cease-and-desist letter. It was successful.

Prosecutor: Did there come a time when the interest in Stormy Daniels' story increased?
A: Yes

Davidson: Donald Trump's notoriety was growing. There was the Access Hollywood tape, the hot mic. It increased interest in Stormy Daniels' story. I wrote, Trump is f-ed. Dylan replied, Wave the white flag, it's over people.
Prosecutor: And the next day?

Davidson: TheDirty republished the story. Dylan said, it could get worse, if Stormy made comments... The moral of the story was, Gina and Dylan came to terms at $120,000 - But AMI would not go forward.

Davidson: Dylan asked Gina to call Cohen, she refused. She asked me call Cohen. I didn't want to.

Prosecutor: Break that down?

Davidson: Bottom line, no one wanted to talk to Michael Cohen.

Davidson: Gina told me, We have this deal, it's going to be the easiest deal you ever had in your life [laughs apparently ruefully], she said, all you have to do is talk to that as*hole Michael Cohen. $10,000 was tacked on for me

Prosecutor: People's 63.

Davidson: It's my email to Cohen, and my firm's wiring instructions.
Prosecutor: Who were the parties?

Davidson: Stormy Daniels versus RCI - an LLC that Michael told me he was going to use to pay for this deal. Resolution Consultants. Peggy Peterson, David Denison

Prosecutor: Is David Denison a real person?

Davidson: Yes. He was on my high school hockey team.
Prosecutor: How does he feel about you now?
Davidson: He's very angry about it

Davidson: Only the side letter agreement identified the parties. And only Michael Cohen kept a copy of the side letter agreement.
Prosecutor: Is that rare?

Davidson: Yes.
Prosecutor: Did you get paid by the deadline?
Davidson: No. So I sent this email

Davidson: Cohen told me, he couldn't send because of firewalls. Then that, "My guy is in four to five states today." It was clear, Cohen didn't have the authority to spend money. Finally he said, "I'll just do it myself."

Prosecutor: Did you think the money was from him?

Davidson: Not until funding.

Prosecutor: Who did you think the money was coming from?

Trump's lawyer: Objection!

Justice Merchan: Overruled.

Davidson: Donald Trump or some corporate connection

Davidson: So I wrote to all of them and said, I'm out, go in peace
Prosecutor: How did Stormy Daniels react?
Davidson: I'm not going to answer that based on attorney client privilege.

Prosecutor: OK. Did you get involved again?
Davidson: Yes. But I don't know how

Davidson: I thought Cohen was trying to kick it down the road until after the election.
Justice Merchan: OK, our afternoon break.
[Jurors leave. Note: Bove is to the right of Trump - seems he'll be doing the cross - WHEN they get to it]
Thread will continue here

[They're back]

Prosecution: Mr. Davidson, have you testified on this in the grand jury?
Trump's lawyer: Objection!
Justice Merchan: Overruled. Please approach

[whispered sidebar ensues. Trump sits alone at defense table, his head cocked to the right]

[They emerge]
Prosecutor: Who did you think was really paying?

Davidson: I find that question confusing.

Prosecutor: When you were dealing with Michael Cohen did you have an understanding about how this deal was doing to be funded?

Davidson: I had an assumption

Prosecutor: To what did you attribute the lack of funding at this point?

Davidson: Frugality.

Prosecutor: Whose frugality?

Trump's lawyer: Objection! May I be heard at the sidebar?

[And again. Susan Necheles, too, at defense table]

Prosecutor: People's 176, these text messages...
Davidson: Dylan wrote, Going to see Pecker in 15,
will ask for an update.
Prosecutor: Did you respond?

Davidson: Yes. I said, Waiting for a call any
second.
Prosecutor: From who(m)?

Davidson: I don't remember

Prosecutor: In sending to Michael Cohen, what
domain did you use?
Davidson: Gmail dot com
Prosecutor: What did you send?

Davidson: Wiring instructions. He told me, We're
sending it. I said, I don't believe you. That, he sent
from trumporg dot org, cc-ing his gmail

Davidson: This was 16 days after the agreement.
Then this email from First Republic, which he
forwarded to me. I meant nothing to me. He had

my wiring instructions - but he didn't send
Prosecutor: Did you speak with him on the phone?
Davidson: He was pants on fire

Davidson: Michael Cohen was talking out of both
ears.
Justice Merchan: We will break here, until
Thursday at 10 am, jurors.
[Jurors leave]
Justice Merchan: I'd like you here at 9:30 on
Thursday.

II. Trump Trial, May 2, 2024

In the Trump trial before Keith Davidson retook the witness stand, Justice Merchan asked to hear about contempt.

The prosecutor focused on Trump's praise of David Pecker as a "nice guy," calling it carrot and stick.

Justice Merchan said he was most concerned about comments about the jury being 95% Democrats and presumptively unfair. Trump's lawyer Todd Blanche said that wasn't about any particular juror. A decision will come.

When Trump's lawyer Emil Bove -- pronounced "Beau-vee" all now agree -- got to cross examine Davidson, the sparks flew.

He asked if Davidson hadn't been investigated for possible extortion in Florida, and about his role in leaking the Lindsay Lohan rehab tape, and Hulk Hogan sex tape.

Davidson took to saying, I don't recall. He tried to push back and say if Bove was, as he said, not trying to play lawyer game, he shouldn't use terms like extract, as in extract money from Charlie Sheen.

By lunch Bove said he had an hour left.

Some said that the defendant chose to hire other dubious characters, of course these are the witnesses against him. But unlike Michael Cohen, who he hired, Trump did not hire Keith Davidson. Now will the wider world of Davidson being investigated for extortion, and his far-flung role in scandals, give the jurors pause? And what about Michael Cohen?

The trial day:

Trump has arrived, now whispering to Todd Blanche to his right in the lead counsel's seat. Seems contempt motion will be argued by Blanche, nor Bove or Necheles.

All rise!

Clerk: This is the People of the State of New York against Donald J. Trump.

Justice Mechan: We'll have our hearing on contempt. The defense provided close to 500 pages in total. People, why don't you go through each of the violations and explain?

Prosecutor: The defendant is claiming that the order was not intended to allow others to attack him without him being able to respond. But he's already been found to have violated the order nine times and he's done it again.

Prosecutor: The Defendant said, The jury was picked very fast, it's a 95% Democrat area. His justification is that the media is saying that. But he amplifies it and creates an air of menace. He places this process in jeopardy.

Prosecutor: On April 25, reporters were questioning him, I think it was all part of the plan, they asked about David Pecker, the defendant said, He's a nice guy. This is classic carrot and stick. He selectively responded to this question and not others

Prosecutor: In an interview to a Pennsylvania TV station on April 23, he said, Michael Cohen is a convicted liar and he has no credibility. He got in trouble, he did some bad things with banking. This was willful and knowing

Prosecutor: On April 22, outside the door to this courtroom in the little pen that's set up, he stood there for 9 minutes and spoke about a witness that will be here at some date in the future, Michael Cohen. He said, Cohen wasn't very good... He got caught lying

Prosecutor: We understand the Court's concern about Michael Cohen. They filed 500 pages, TikToks, but there's nothing to indicate Defendant saw these when they were made. Michael Cohen is not a political opponent. There is an order, and these are violations

Prosecutor: Mr. Blanche right here said that his client understands the gag order. So we have met our burden. We are asking for the maximum $1000 payments. We are not yet seeking jail, to avoid disruption to this proceeding.

Justice Merchan: Mr. Blanche?

Trump's lawyer Todd Blanche: On Tuesday, the Court said to us that the purpose of the gag order is to shield those fearful of reprisal from the Defendant- that's a reason to deny these four. You've said your order is not intended to allow unfettered attacks on him

Trump's lawyer Blanche: Since President Trump announced in '22, almost two years ago, there have been attacks by Michael Cohen and people he has on his podcast.
Justice Merchan: My main concern is with conduct after the gag order was issued.

Trump's lawyer Blanche: I will focus on recent statements. Last week President Trump's rival, President Biden said in a public forum, he talked about a witness in this trial, he said, You might call it Stormy weather. President Trump can't respond due to the gag

Justice Merchan: He can respond to President Biden. He just can't speak about a witness in this trial.

Trump's lawyer Blanche: But President Biden can... These exhibits are mostly tweets or retweets by Michael Cohen, recents, and podcasts, also recent

Trump's lawyer Blanche: There may be a need to remove some people from the gag order if they don't need protecting. On Pecker, President Trump said on April 23 for a news show in Philadelphia answering on Pecker. President Trump was factual and neutral, no warning

Trump's lawyer Blanche: President Trump has known Mr. Pecker for decades-

Justice Merchan: It's not just about Mr. Pecker, it's the message to other witnesses. I have expressed my concerns about Mr. Cohen. But it's about the other witnesses, that's a concern

Trump's lawyer Blanche: Every word that's being said here is being reported, in real time. President Trump has to respond. What's happening in this trial -

Justice Merchan: It's not surprising we have press here. The defendant is the former president

Justice Merchan: The defendant is the leading Republican candidate, now... I don't have the authority over the press. I can't extend the gag order to them. Let me ask you, when your client went to that holding area - he went to them, not the press to him.

Trump's lawyer Blanche: I agree, but President Trump has to be able to speak, he's running.

Justice Merchan: That is why the area is set up. He can speak about the DA of NY county.
Blanche: On Pecker, what President Trump said was that he was nice. That's all.

Justice Merchan: I'm not terribly concerned with that one.
Trump's lawyer Blanche: Mr. Cohen has been inviting, almost daring President Trump to respond to him. Let me put some on the screen-
Justice Merchan: Hurry.
[On screen, photos of Trump in orange, & Mandela

Trump's lawyer Blanche: Here, Mr. Cohen says he won't send money to President Trump's commissary account in jail, then something obnoxious...
[Photo of Barry Diller, Squawkbox, Meidas - now down]
Blanche: Mr. Cohen has been shopping a TV show

Justice Merchan: We've made your point.
Trump's lawyer Blanche: Cohen has interviewed reporters in this room who blast President Trump for what he did while he was President- in excess of 10, way in excess of 10. Mr. Cohen goes on TikTok nightly, making money

Trump's lawyer Blanche: This is not a man who needs protection from the gag order.
Justice Merchan: What about the comments made about the jury?
Blanche: It was 15 second from a 20-minute interview. This trial matters to voters. We believe this is political

Justice Merchan: He said the jury was rushed through. Does this violate the gag order?
Trump's lawyer Blanche: He wasn't speaking about a particular juror, if they are Democrat - the press has done that.
Justice Merchan: It's 10:10, let's wrap it up.

Blanche: Stormy Daniels does not need to be protected by this gag order.
Justice Merchan: Jury in 5 minutes.

Jury entering!

Prosecutor: Mr. Davidson, you were talking about your emails with and about Michael Cohen. People's Exhibit 168, please blow it up. What does it say?
Davidson: Executed agreement, changed to correct LLC. Escrow until receipt of agreement. By Dylan

Prosecutor: What was this email about?
Davidson: We'd had a phone call. I'd lost trust in Michael Cohen. Dylan then mediated.

Prosecutor: Why did you lose trust with Michael Cohen?

Davidson: He was not telling me the truth -
Prosecutor: OK!

Prosecutor: And this one, you produced under subpoena, what does it say?

Davidson: List Essential Consultants LLC...Your, Michael Cohen.

Prosecutor: Did you respond?

Davidson: Yes, at 7:02 am. I said, I will work in good faith

Prosecutor: Did you receive the funds as a wire from Essential Consultants?
Davidson: Yes.

Prosecutor: And this on liquidated damages, what does it mean?
Davidson: I authored this provision. It was for $1 million per violation.

Davidson: I believe this provision would be unenforceable. But Michael Cohen demanded it.

Prosecutor: Who is DD?

Davidson: Donald Trump.

Prosecutor: Is his name written here in the side letter?

Davidson: Yes, that's my handwriting. It says Attorney's Eyes Only

Prosecutor: Who signed for David Denison?
Davidson: Michael Cohen.
Prosecutor: How much did you personally make from this deal?
Davidson: $10,000.

Prosecutor: How much to Stormy Daniels?
Davidson: I feel that invades attorney client privilege.

Prosecutor: When the article came out about Karen McDougal's agreement, how did Michael Cohen react?

Davidson: He was angry, about the timing, just before the election.
Prosecutor: And this, on the election night, what did you write?
Davidson: What have we done?

Prosecutor: What did you mean?
Davidson: That we have may helped get Donald Trump elected.
Prosecutor: What did Dylan Howard respond with?
Davidson: OMG - oh my God.

Prosecutor: Who won the election?
Davidson: Donald Trump

Davidson: Later Michael Cohen called me, I was in a strangely decorated department store, he said, Jesus Christ, can you f*cking believe I'm not going to DC, after everything I'd done for that f*cking guy, I've saved his a*s so many times. He didn't pay me $130K

Prosecutor: Is this a receipt from the store you were in when you got the call from Michael Cohen?
Davidson: Yes. December 9, 2016.
Prosecutor: I'm almost afraid to ask, but how was the store decorated?
Davidson: It was a big box, like Alice in Wonderland

Prosecution: Now to early 2018, what's this?
Davidson: I had received a comment call from the WSJ, about Stormy Daniels and Donald Trump. I reiterated our 2011 denial, our cease and desist letter to The Dirty dot com. It was Jan 10, 2018. I forwarded to Cohen

Prosecutor: I'll show you People's exhibit 255. What is it?
Davidson: Instant messages between me and Michael Cohen. I wrote, WSJ called Stormy,

deadline tonight. Cohen responded, Write a strong denial for her, like you did before.

Prosecution: Was what was issued true?

Davidson: Technically.

Prosecution: How?

Davidson: The relationship was not romantic.

Prosecution: But sexual?

Davidson: It was and/or

Prosecution: So it was cleverly worded?

Davidson: I don't understand the question

Davidson: You call it hush money, I call it consideration, a settlement in a civil matter.

Prosecutor: You wouldn't call it hush money?
Davidson: I would never use that work. I call it consideration.

Davidson: Cohen was text me... Stormy was going to go on Hannity... Then he wrote back, no interviews. It was another of his pants-on-fire moments, he asked someone or some wisemen, they said, no interviews.

Prosecution: What does this text say?

Davidson: Cohen asks, Why is she going on Kimmel after SOTU? I replied, IDK. It was difficult - she might have to repay the money, and liquidated damages. Stormy said, This is my shot. She wanted to rejuvenate her career

Prosecution: You don't have to read all of these, but what is it about?
Davidson: A news article that had been published. I was receiving hundreds of phone calls.

Prosecution: Did you prepare another denial before Kimmel?
Davidson: Another statement

Prosecutor: Where were you when you typed this statement?

Davidson: I was in the Marilyn Monroe suite in the Roosevelt Hotel in Hollywood California. There were hair people there Gina Rodriguez and her then boyfriend Anthony.

Prosecutor: Why there?

Davidson: Kimmel booked the suite for Stormy. The statement ended, Please check me out on Instagram.

Prosecutor: How was it true, denying an alleged sexual relationship?

Davidson: It was not a relationship. That'd mean an ongoing interaction

Prosecutor: What are these texts?

Davidson: Cohen was watching Kimmel, he texted me, She is saying it's not her signature. He asked me, Did you say she signed it in front of you?

Prosecutor: What did you reply?

Davidson: WTF. It's an expression of exasperation

Prosecutor: And what next?

Davidson: Gina said she was mad at Stormy, that Stormy had her look like a liar. Gina said she's have a long talk with Stormy on the plane to New York. They were going to film something.

Prosecutor: Did Michael Cohen threaten a suit?

Davidson: Many times. He can be a very aggressive guy. He threatened to rain down legal hell on Stormy. He'd say, You don't know who you are f*cking him.
Prosecutor: What did you want you to do?
Davidson: Deny

Prosecutor: Whose contacts did Cohen sent you?
Davidson: Christopher Cuomo.
Prosecutor: Who is he?
Davidson: He's in the broadcasting business.
Prosecutor: What did you write?
Davidson: That Cohen having paid was in conformity with what he told me.

Prosecutor: Did you check it with Mr. Cohen then send it to Christopher Cuomo?

Davidson: Yes. And I believe it was truthful. It was what Cohen had told me: "F*ck it, I'll just do it myself," he'd said.

Prosecutor: But you believe that the ultimate source of funds was Mr. Trump?
Davidson: At the time of the transaction... Later in the department store conversation, he said he had not been reimbursed.

Prosecutor: Do you have a stake in this trial?
Davidson: No
Prosecutor: No further questions
Justice Merchan: We'll take a break.

[They've back]
All rise!
Trump's lawyer Emil Bove ("bovee") Good morning, Mr. Davidson. You've never met President Trump, right?
Davidson: I have not.
Bove: You only know of Mr. Trump from TV and Michael Cohen, right?
Davidson: And some other clients. Not from him

Trump's lawyer Bove: You got other AMI business through Dylan Howard, right? A labor matter with a reporter?

Davidson: Yes, a California matter, I consulted
Bove: You testified to the grand jury, in 2023, and
said Ms. McDougal didn't want to publish?
Davidson: Yes

Trump's lawyer Bove: Ms. McDougal had had a
real career, on magazine covers, right?

Davidson: More than that.

Bove: You called her AMI deal a dream deal?

Davidson: She called it that.
Bove: You didn't discuss that with Michael Cohen
until it closed?
Davidson: Yes

Trump's lawyer Bove: You had a reciprocal referral
relationship with Gina Rodriguez?

Davidson: Somewhat...

Bove: You tried to represent her in this matter?

Davidson: I returned a call for her.

Bove: But the DA's office told you it was a conflict?

Davidson: I disagree

Davidson: I didn't agree , but did not represent Ms. Rodriguez.

Trump's lawyer Bove: You represented Stormy Daniels in her $130,000 agreement, right?

Davidson: Yes.

Bove: The word "decoded" was used - it was your idea, right?
Davidson: No. It's widely used

Trump's lawyer Bove: In the Alice in Wonderland warehouse conversation, Michael Cohen was down?

Davidson: I thought he was going to kill himself.

Bove: He'd told you he thought he'd be chief of staff, or Attorney General, right?
Davidson: He had.

Trump's lawyer Bove: When you met with the DA's Office, it was by Zoom and Mark Pomerantz asked the questions, right?
Davidson: Yes.
Prosecution: Objection!
[Sidebar]
Justice Merchan: Sustained.
Bove: What does extortion mean to you?

Davidson: Coercion, and more

Trump's lawyer Bove: It is your believe that the statute of limitations has expired on any extortion by you in this case?

Davidson: I haven't thought of that.
Bove: You're a lawyer and you haven't thought of that, prior to your testimony?

Davidson: I have not.

Trump's lawyer Bove: Do you remember telling the DA's office that you didn't recall the election being the deadline?

Davidson: I recall saying "I do not recall."

Bove: You say you worked on media cases - with NDAs, right?

Davidson: Right.

Trump's lawyer Bove: You were pretty well versed in getting right up to the line without it become extortion?

Davidson: I don't know what you mean.

Bove: You familiarized yourself with extortion law based on a particular experience, right?

Davidson: No.

Trump's lawyer Bove: Weren't you investigated for extortion under Florida law in 2012?

Davidson: Yes.

Bove: So you tried to avoid extortion about the 2016 elections, to Michael Cohen?
Davidson: No...

Trump's lawyer Bove: You represented Dawn Holland leaking about Lindsay Lohan in rehab, TMZ paid her $10,000?

Davidson: I don't recall.
Bove: She was your client, yes?
Davidson: I don't know what you are referring to.
Bove: You brokered the Tila Tequila sex tape?

Trump's lawyer Bove: You were on a 90 day Bar suspension?

Davidson: I don't recall.

Bove: You extracted money from Charlie Sheen, right?

Davidson: There's no extraction.

Bove: You caused Charlie Sheen to pay.
Davidson: There was tortious behavior

Trump's lawyer Bove: You got a client to sign a 60% retainer agreement, when she could barely complete a sentence, on meth?
Prosecution: Objection!

Justice Merchan: Sustained.

Bove: You're fuzzy?

Davidson: I've had 1500 clients.

Bove: What about Capri Anderson?

Davidson: Assuming *arguendo* -
Trump's lawyer Bove: We're both lawyers. I'm not here to play legal games - I just want truthful answers.

Davidson: You're getting truthful answers. And if you're not here to play legal games, don't use words like "extract."

Trump's lawyer Bove: Did Capri Anderson reach a settlement with Charlie Sheen?

Davidson: I am not going to answer that question.
Bove: Your Honor, please instruct the witness to answer.
Justice Merchan: He's asserting privilege. Ask another question.

Trump's lawyer Bove: What about the Hulk Hogan tape - did you tell him the Gawker post was just a shot across the bow?

Davidson: I do not recall that.
Bove: Let's go to a People's exhibit, messages with Michael Cohen - about Hulk Hogan?
Davidson: I see it.

Trump's lawyer Bove: You told Hulk Hogan's representation you didn't want to out gay men, that they should pay, you demanded money?
Davidson: I made a monetary demand, yes.
Bove: Then the National Enquirer published? Look at Defense Exhibit F2-7, for the parties

Trump's lawyer Bove: Didn't Dylan Howard have a byline on one of the Hulk Hogan tape articles?

Davidson: Yes.
Bove: You gave the info to Dylan Howard?
Davidson: I did not.

Bove; There was an FBI investigation of this, right?
Davidson: Yes.

Trump's lawyer Bove: The FBI had a sting operation?

Davidson: I don't know what that is.
Bove: The FBI was recording you, a couple of doors down.
Davidson; They had an investigation.
Bove: The Tampa PD referenced extortion?
Davidson: They investigated

Trump's lawyer Bove: You became familiar with extortion law?
Davidson: Perhaps.
Bove: And in the Manny Pacquiao finder's fee case, you said if there was no settlement, the guy would never find work in California?
Davidson: I don't speak like that.

Trump's lawyer Bove: Back to this case. A friend of Karen McDougal was trying to publicize Ms. McDougal's relationship without her consent?

Davidson: I didn't know who.

Bove: Your fee was 45%

Davidson: Yes.

Bove: You mentioned John Crawford?

Davidson: Ex PD

Trump's lawyer Bove: Crawford also owns UPS
stores around Phoenix?
Davidson: I believe so

Bove: Crawford got paid?

Davidson: Yes he was compensated.

Bove: You know California rules prohibit non
attorneys being paid from attorney's fees? You've
been disciplined?
No

Trump's lawyer Bove: You garnered confidence by
already gotten interest from the National Enquirer -
you told Karen McDougal that?
Davidson: Perhaps.

Trump's lawyer Bove: So you're relationship with
Dylan Howard benefited your law practice, right?
Davidson: I don't see how the two are related
Bove: But AMI said Ms. McDougal had not
provided enough evidence - so you wrote to Dylan
she found her Blackberry

Bove: You told Mr. Howard you were drafting a
declination letter?
Davidson: I don't recall.
Justice Merchan: Let's break.

[They've back]

Justice Merchan: Anything before we bring the
jurors in?
Trump's lawyer Necheles: I am handing up articles
that President Trump would like to post on his
Truth Social. But they mention witnesses and
prosecutors - the gag is order ambiguous

Prosecutor: They are asking for advance rulings.
Sure there is a political campaign. But there is a
criminal trial here.
Justice Merchan: I'm not going to issue an advance
ruling. I'd say, be cautious.

Trump's lawyer Necheles: He want to argue it's political

Justice Merchan: I'd say, Steer clear. Get the jury.

[Jury entering]

Trump's lawyer Bove: Gina Rodriguez' boyfriend Anthony, he wrote the piece on The Dirty, right?

Davidson: I don't know.

Bove: And The Dirty is owned by Karen McDougal's ex?
Davidson: Don't know

Trump's lawyer Bove: You were able to get the 2011 The Dirty post taken down because Gina Rodriguez' boyfriend wrote it?

Davidson: She could have just told her boyfriend.

Bove: This cease and desist letter wasn't one of

your big victories?
Davidson: It worked

Trump's lawyer Bove: Didn't Larry Flint offer to indemnify Stormy Daniels about the settlement agreement, right?

Davidson: I think there were other terms too.
Bove: But her legal fees would have been paid.
Davidson: It's still problem in one's life

Trump's lawyer Bove: You kept working with Michael Cohen, after Stormy - he sent you a client?

Davidson: He sent me a non-paying client.
Bove: What about Summer Zervos? And Shera Bechard who claimed sex with Elliott Broid

Davidson: I don't recall.
Trump's lawyer Bove: You don't remember this morning? They asked if Mr. Cohen had ever recorded your conversations?

Davidson: Some agency asked. I said Yes - his conversations were odd at times - he was speaking, then, in a linear fashion

Trump's lawyer Bove: Please put on the headphones
[He does, with hand raised. Light blue suit]
Bove: That was your voice, right?
Davidson: Yes.
Bove: And you spoke about "settlers remorse" and leverage, about Stormy Daniels, correct?
Davidson: Probably.

Trump's lawyer Bove: When you said "hypothetically speaking," that was code, right? So you could sit in a chair like this and say, "I'm not sure" and "Probably"?

Davidson: No.
Bove: It was Stormy Daniels' goal, wasn't it, to create leverage over President Trump?

Davidson: I think you are grossly misstating -
Trump's lawyer Bove: There's no question pending.

Prosecutor: Let him answer.

Justice Merchan: You may answer.
Davidson: You are misstating the time period.
Bove: Then Stormy hired Michael Avenatti, right?

Davidson: Yes.

Trump's lawyer Bove: And you said, "Michael Avenatti is really driving a wedge between Stormy and Gina."
Davidson: I don't entirely recall.
Bove: You can listen to it. Put on the headphones. [Does]

Trump's lawyer Bove: Now do you remember?

Davidson: Yes.
Bove: Did you say that it was not discussed, if Donald Trump was paying Michael Cohen back?

Davidson: I do not recall.
[More audio played, only for the parties and witness]

Davidson: It's true.
Trump's lawyer Bove: Did you say to Michael Cohen, We both want the truth out there?

Davidson: Yes.

Bove: In April 2018 did you speak with Michael Cohen about Gina Rodriguez and her boyfriend, what he was saying?
Davidson: No.

Trump's lawyer Bove: Do you recall telling Mr. Cohen a quote, that if he loses the election and he will this story is worth zero, we have no f-ing leverage?
Davidson: Yes.
Bove: For everyone, the agreement - this is a legal document?
Davidson: Yes.

Trump's lawyer Bove: You even had copyright in here.
Davidson: Transfer of copyright.
Bove: And on this signature page, David Dennison had not signed, correct?
Davidson: He had not.

Bove: And you do not know what happened to this after you saw it?
Davidson: No.
Bove: No further questions.
Justice Merchan: Cross?

Prosecutor: Can I have five minutes?
Justice Merchan: Let's break.

[They've back]
Prosecutor Steinglass: Mr. Bove asked you about conversations with Michael Cohen- had Michael Avenatti taken Stormy Daniels as a client, and sued both of you?
Davidson: Yes
Prosecutor: So were you saying Stormy Daniels was not threatened in LV?
No.

Prosecutor: The quote, "If he loses the election we lose all f*cking leverage" - who said it?

Davidson: Anthony.

Prosecutor: Let's display People's 267 while playing 265...

[Audio of Cohen: Would you write a book? Would you break away from Trump doctrine?

[Audio on Cohen continues, "No one is thinking about Michael... What about me? How many times he's said to me, I hate that we did it. And I told him, it was the right move. Davidson (on audio) Even if you let to write a book, you probably couldn't. MC: Nah, I could

Prosecutor: What did it mean, I hate that we did it?

Davidson: The Stormy Daniels settlement.
Prosecutor Steinglass: No further questions.

Justice Merchan: Mr. Bove?
Trump's lawyer Bove: You don't know the date of this, right?
Davidson: I do not

Trump's lawyer Bove: We move these into evidence [no objection] play them
[On audio: Davidson on "settler's remorse," settle by date X or no leverage - or you try to settle twice, if you get a chance (pause) hypothetically speaking]
Bove: Next audio clip

[On audio, Davidson said: Gina brought Stormy to Avenatti... The $130,000, was there ever any indication that the money was coming from him? And I said, No. They said, Did you ever ask? I said, I don't ask other lawyers about their conversations

[Audio continues: Davidson said, It's going to air later today. We both know it's the truth, Michael.]
Bove: Next audio clip
[On audio: "Stormy said, if he loses the case and we lose leverage, I'm going to sue you. That's called being pushed into settling a case]

Trump's lawyer Bove: DD, you say it was Donald Trump, a man you've never met, never been in the same room with until this Tuesday, right?
Davidson: That is true.
Bove: No further questions.

Justice Merchan: Next witness.

The People call Douglas Daus [custodial witness]
Prosecutor: Tell me about your history.
Daus: I was in Iraq from 2009 and 2011, tech work.

Prosecutor: At DANY, what are you?
Daus: Computer and film tech expert, supervising analyst. I keep up with technology

Prosecutor: How many devices have you analyzed while at HTAU [DANY's High Technology Analysis Unit]?
Daus: 3,392

Prosecutor: More or less.

Daus: More or less.
Prosecutor: Did you extract Michael Cohen's Apple
6S and Apple 7?
Daus: Yes.

Prosecutor: Did you note the last four numbers of
the cell phone's number?

Daus: 0114
[Serial numbers too...]
Prosecutor: I move to admit these exhibits
Justice Merchan: No objections? It's entered into
evidence.

Prosecutor: Let's pull up an example. Who are
these text messages between?
Daus: Michael Cohen and Hope Hicks.
Prosecutor: What are the last 4 of her number?
Daus: 0226

Prosecutor: How many contacts did Michael Cohen
have?
Daus: 39,745. A lot.

Prosecutor: Have you ever met Michael Cohen?
Daus: Yes. I mean, no. I've seen him.

Prosecutor: How?
Daus: I watch a lot of news.

Prosecutor: And this audio file?
Daus: It's with Keith Davidson, in Voice Notes
Prosecutor: People's 247
Daus: It's from 9/6/16

Prosecutor: And People's Exhibit 246 - is this a
transcript of the last 46 seconds and is it accurate?
Daus: Yes.
[Audio is played: Trump saying "let me know
what's happening, okay?... it's such bullshit... I
think this goes away quickly." Cohen: Big time]

[More audio: Cohen: I need to set up a company for
the transfer, our friend David...]
Prosecutor: Nothing further.
Justice Merchan: Cross?
Trump's lawyer Bove: You said your work in Iraq
was similar to for DANY.
Daus: Yes.
Bove: But this is for a criminal case.

Trump's lawyer Bove: These hashes are long - so the computer does it for you, right?

Daus: Correct.

Bove: You testified today about some of the artifacts from 2 phones - segments of much broader data, right?

Daus: Yes. I'm not part of the investigative team

Justice Merchan: We'll break now. And tomorrow we'll break at 3:45. Jurors, do not read about the case.

[Jurors leave]

III. Trump Trial, May 3, 2024: Hope

On Friday in the Trump trial, former press secretary Hope Hicks took the stand, under subpoena.

She had gone from publicizing Ivanka Trump's personal brand to fielding emails seeking comment on the Access Hollywood tape to the catch-and-kill journalism of the National Enquirer's David Pecker.

Like Pecker, she offered praise to Trump, describing relationships of his as "respectful" and praising his media savvy.

As Trump's best cross-examiner (so far) Emil Bove slipping into the lead counsel's seat, one wondered how this cross examination might go.

The prosecution, though, must have liked that she described Trump as running everything, and everyone reporting to him.

Earlier in the trial, this appears to have been their point in introducing into evidence a document showing him managing his own Winged Foot golf course renewals.

Also earlier on Friday, Justice Merchan made a point of countering the argument that if Trump does not testify, his gag order is to blame.

On Thursday after Justice Merchan's comments on the gag order, Trump's lawyer Susan Necheles handed up a slew of article she said Trump would like to retweet. But could he, if they mentioned a prosecutor by name? When in doubt, don't, Justice Merchan said. Then on Friday, he said there are no restriction on what could be said - about witnesses or jurors - from the witness stand.

Trial Day May 3, 2024

Trump has arrived - blue suit, blue tie - and is talking to his lawyer Emil Bove to his right in the lead counsel / cross examination seat. Blanche crosses aisle to confer with prosecution. Drum roll.

All rise!
Clerk: This is the People of the State of New York versus Donald J. Trump.
Justice Merchan: Before we put the witness on the stand, I want to clarify to Mr. Trump that you have an absolute right to testify at trial.

Justice Merchan: The order restricting extrajudicial statements does not limit what you can say from the stand. That's why it's called "extrajudicial" statement.
Trump's lawyer Blanche: We have evidentiary objections about the next witness. There is hearsay

Trump's lawyer Blanche: The People are trying to introduce a full transcript of the Access Hollywood tape - but it is only coming in to show intent. Mr. Pecker already testified about it. I expect there will be a witness today who was speak extensively about it

Trump's lawyer Blanche: The Court would take into account the Weinstein decision -

Justice Merchan: You mean the reversal on Harvey Weinstein? I don't think that ruling changes my view at all. The law of Sandoval remains the same.

Trump's lawyer Blanche: Then there's the Truth [Social] about If you come after me, I'm covering after you. There's been briefing in DC, the gag order there - but there's no proof. Maybe they came prove up on other tweets.

Justice Merchan: The jury is waiting

Prosecutor: The Court ruled we can introduce a transcript of the Access Hollywood tape - can we do it with the photo blacked out? It's from the Wayback Machine.

Justice Merchan: The People do have a right to establish the date when it was published

Justice Merchan: Let's get the witness, and then the jury
[Dau takes stand, is told he's still under oath; jury enters

Trump's lawyer Emil Bove: The two cell phones, you got the consent of Michael Cohen, signed Jan 19, 2023?
Daus: Yes.
Bove: But you got it Jan 23

Trump's lawyer Bove: Your unit didn't get the two phones under January 23. Let's talk about chain of custody - there's only 1 signature as witness, not two - that's not ideal if there is a dispute, right?
Daus: Theoretically.
Bove: You'd want to have 2 witnesses

Trump's lawyer Bove: You don't know if the phone was hooked up to the Internet, do you?
Daus: I do not.
Bove: You found a Signal App on the phone, yes?
Daus: I did.
Bove: Self-delete is an option, and it is difficult to get them then?
Daus: It is.

Trump's lawyer Bove: Mr. Cohen had it set for messages to self-destruct in 7 seconds?
Daus: He did.
Bove: What about the Dust app, which allows self-delete as soon as a message is read - it would make it impossible for someone like to you reconstruct?
Daus: Yes

Trump's lawyer Bove: A factor re-set can wipe all the data off a phone, right?
Daus: It can.
Bove: There was a factory re-set of Michael Cohen's phone in October 2016, yes?
Daus: There was.
Bove: So where did the file come from? On January 25, 2017, a sync

Trump's lawyer Bove: You don't know what the back-up entailed?
Daus: That file, certainly.
Bove: We'll talk about the September 6 file. But first, you didn't collect Michael Cohen's laptop?
Daus: We did not.
Bove: That's how you could know what he loaded on

Trump's lawyer Bove: The large number of contacts could come from the sync, right?
Daus: It could.
Bove: You know the call was cut off?
Daus: Near the end.
Bove: How do you know it was the end? Bring up Defense G19 - does it refresh your recollection?
Daus: No

Trump's lawyer Bove: The call you say came in at the end of the audio file - there's nothing on the cell

phone about it, is there?
Daus: There is not.
Bove: This photo of Michael Cohen in the White House, is this the meta data?
Daus: Yes.

Trump's lawyer Bove: But there's no similar meta data for the audio files?
Daus: There is not.
Bove: There was another sync in October - but the exhibits show nothing about it - so we just have to take Michael Cohen's word about that happened in October 2020

Trump's lawyer Bove: And the phone was turned on again in 2022, did you know?
Daus: I did not.
Bove: And Michael Cohen used it to make another recording - and you don't know what he did-
Prosecution: Objection!
Justice Merchan: Sustained

Trump's lawyer Bove: So we just have to take Michael Cohen's word for it?
Daus: We do.
Bove: No further questions.
Justine Merchan: Re-direct?
Prosecutor Chris Conroy: You don't hang out with

Michael Cohen, do you?
Daus: I do not

Prosecutor Conroy: And you actually saw no evidence of tampering, did you?
Daus: I did not
Conroy: No further questions.
(re-cross) Bove: You saw the possibility of tampering - and the cut off of the file by a call, nothing on that in the phone, right?
Daus: Right

Justice Merchan: Counsel, please approach. [Whispered sidebar; seats on either side of Trump at defense table are empty, Susan Necheles 1 seat down]
Justice Merchan: Next witness?
Prosecutor: The People call Georgia Longstreet [of DANY]

Prosecutor: Where do you work?
Longstreet: DANY. I'm a paralegal.
Prosecutor: Have you worked on a case against Donald Trump?
Longstreet: Yes. For about the last year and a half.
Prosecutor: Collecting social media info?
Longstreet: Tweet, Instagram, Truth Social

Prosecutor: How many social media posts have you saved?
Longstreet: 1500. I use SnagIt then I hash it.
Prosecutor: Did you review [at] RealDonaldTrump on Twitter?
Longstreet: I did. And [at] POTUS45.
Prosecutor: What is Truth Social?
Longstreet: It's like Twitter

Prosecutor: Did you use the WayBack Machine to review previously published news articles?
Longstreet: I did.
Prosecutor: Including 405A, the Washington Post article [Access Hollywood tape]
Trump's lawyer Blanche: Objection
Justice Merchan: Jurors, step out

[With jury out]
Trump's lawyer Blanche: We'd like to discuss a stipulation [about exhibit], given your ruling
Justice Merchan: I'm going to step out for a few minutes.
Thread will continue here

[They've back]
Justice Merchan: I'm satisfied a foundation has been laid by the witness for authenticity.
Prosecutor: Your Honor ruled that we can introduce evidence to offset defendant's claim the

witnesses benefit from testifying, and to explain previous denials

[Jury entering]
Prosecutor: We have a stipulation that the Access Hollywood tape was published by the Washington Post on Oct 7, 2016. We offer these exhibits.
Trump's lawyer Blanche: Objection.
Justice Merchan: Objection is noted.
Prosecutor: 407A

[Jury is shown video of Trump apologizing for Access Hollywood tape: "This is a distraction. I've said some foolish things. Bill Clinton has actually abused women, and Hillary has intimidated his victims."]
Prosecutor: When was this?
Longstreet: October 8, 2016

Prosecutor: What's this?
Longstreet: From Truth Social, on March 15, 2023: "I did nothing wrong in the Horse Face case... felon, jailbird Michael Cohen." Then, "IF YOU GOT AFTER ME, I'M COMING AFTER YOU!!"
Prosecutor: No further questions.

Cross-examination.
Trump's lawyer Blanche: Did you review the Twitter of Michael Cohen?

Longstreet: Yes.
Blanche: Have you reviewed his TIkTok?
Longstreet: No.
Blanche: Listened to all of his "Mea Culpa"
podcasts?
Longstreet: Absolutely not

Trump's lawyer Blanche: You have no independent
knowledge of how Truth Social date stamps its
post?
Longstreet: I do not.
Blanche: No further questions.

Prosecutor: The People call Hope Hicks.

Trump's lawyer: Objection, we-

Justice Merchan: Come up
[sidebar]

Witness: I am Hope Hicks. I started working in
different P.R. and marketing jobs, Hiltzik
Strategies, crisis communications for well-known
individuals. I met Ivanka Trump and started to help
with her personal brand then the Trump hospitality
initiatives

Prosecutor: Did you work for the Trump campaign?

Hicks: Yes. Mr. Trump - at that time, Mister Trump - said he was exploring a campaign.
Prosecutor: What do you do now?

Hicks: I have a communications company.
Prosecutor: Have you been subpoenaed by DANY? Yes.

Prosecutor: Who's paying for your lawyer?
Hicks: I am.
Prosecutor: When did you last speak with the defendant?
Hicks: Summer 2022.
Prosecutor: How did you start with the Trump Organization?
Hicks: It was thriving: gold courses and buildings, Don Jr. and Eric.

Prosecutor: Were you called in to Mr. Trump's office while he was meeting with someone else?

Hicks: Yes. He might call in for poll numbers, positive press about properties.

Prosecutor: Who did you report to?

Hicks: Everyone who works there reports to Mr. Trump

Prosecutor: Are you familiar with Keith Schiller?

Hicks: Mr. Trump's bodyguard. They were close.
Prosecutor: And Rhona Graff?

Hicks: She was crucial to how everything ran on the 26th floor.
[Note: in the lead counsel chair, presumably to cross, is Emil Bove]

Prosecutor: And Allen Weiselberg?

Hicks: All things financial. Mr. Trump lent himself money for the campaign at first.
Prosecutor: Required financial disclosure, tell us about it.
Hicks: We did it and put out a press release.

Prosecutor: Michael Cohen?

Hicks: He was the lawyer.
Prosecutor: Tell us about the campaign.

Hicks: He said, We're going to Iowa. Then New Hampshire and South Carolina. I became the press secretary

Prosecutor: Was Mr. Trump focused on press coverage of the campaign?
Hicks: Yes.
Prosecutor: What phone did you use? Last 4 digits.
Hicks: 0226
Prosecutor: Do you know David Pecker?
Hicks: Yes. Editor of the National Enquirer.

Prosecutor: Do you remember being in a meeting with the two?
Hicks: No.
Prosecutor: Did you hear calls?

Hicks: Yes. There was one after the National Enquirer story about Dr. Ben Carson.

Prosecutor: What about?

Hicks: Medical malpractice.

Hicks: Mr. Trump said it might be Pulitzer Prize worthy. Then there was the story about Ted Cruz' father and Lee Harvey Oswald.

Prosecutor: Did you become aware of the Access Hollywood tape?
Hicks: I got an email from the Washington Post. I was on the 14th floor

Hicks: I forwarded the email to Steve Bannon, Kellyanne Conway, Jason Miller -

Prosecutor: Did you says Deny Deny Deny!

Hicks (laughs) I didn't see that the whole transcript was there. It made the strategy harder.

[Trump is looking down and taking notes]

Hicks: Mr. Trump was doing debate prep, he saw the five of us talking and asked us to come in.

Prosecutor: What did he say?

Hicks: He said that it didn't sound like something that he would say.
Prosecutor: Were you with Mr. Trump when you

saw the video?
A: Yes

Prosecutor: How did he react?

Hicks: He was upset... He knew it wasn't good, but it was locker room talk, pretty standard stuff for two guys chatting with each other.

Prosecutor: What did he say should be done?

Hicks: Yes... We put out a statement.

Hicks: I got the email at 1:30, the story was posted at 3:30 and our statement was out by 4 pm. It said, Bill Clinton has said far worse
Prosecution: Did you post a video?

Hicks: Yes.

[Jury is shown statement Longstreet brought into evidence an hour ago]

Prosecutor: What was the media response?
Hicks: It was intense. It dominated the news cycle until the debate. News about a Category 4 hurricane fell away.

Prosecutor: Did prominent Republicans condemn Mr. Trump?

Hicks: Paul Ryan, Mitt Romney, the usual group

Prosecutor: Did Paul Ryan disinvite Mr. Trump from a campaign event in Wisconsin?

Trump's lawyer Bove: Objection!

Justine Merchan: Overruled.

Prosecutor: Did Mr. Ryan say he was sickened by Mr. Trump?

Hicks: Sounds like something he would say

Prosecutor: And Mitch McConnell - does this refresh your recollection?
Hicks: He said it was repugnant and unacceptable.

Prosecutor: Who was John McCain?

Hicks: He was a Senator

Trump's lawyer Bove: Objection!

Justice Merchan: Sustained.

Prosecutor: Did Speaker Ryan do a call with House members and do you know what he said?

Trump's lawyer Bove: Objection, may I be heard at sidebar?
Justice Merchan: Approach

[After sidebar]

Justice Merchan: The objection is sustained

Prosecutor: Did you reach out to Michael Cohen?

Hicks: Yes, about a rumor that there was another tape out there. I asked him to call a media friend of his.
Prosecutor: Did Mr. Cohen follow up?

Hicks: I think he made the call. There was no such tape.

Hicks: At the debate Sunday in St. Louis, the Access Hollywood tape was among the first questions. After the debate, there were more reports.
Prosecution: Did you attend the rally in Greensboro NC on Oct 15?
Hicks: Yes.
[Jury hears: If 5% believe, we don't win]

Prosecutor: Who could post on [at] RealDonaldTrump?

Hicks: Only Mr. Trump and Dan Scavino.
Prosecution: Had you heard of Karen McDougal?

Hicks: I heard in November 2016.
Prosecutor: And Stormy Daniels?
Hicks: In 2015, about a celebrity golf tournament

Hicks: After I got the email from the WSJ, I thought maybe through Rupert Mudoch we could buy some time. I forwarded it to Jared Kushner, he had a relationship

Prosecutor: We offer this into evidence
Justice Merchan: Admitted

Prosecutor: Did you ask Michael Cohen for input?

Hicks: He edited my draft statement.
Prosecutor: Did you speak with Mr. Trump?

Hicks: He wanted to have an understanding. I told him what Mr. Pecker said to me, that it was a legitimate contract for services

Hicks: He did not want to use the statement we had drafted, he wanted to write his own - a denial and that we didn't know anything about this deal.
Prosecutor: When you learned that Stormy Daniels would also be in the story, did you talk with Mr. Trump?
Yes

Hicks: Yes. He said deny everything. I thought the story was not about....certain behavior.
Justice Merchan: We'll break

They're back; Trump speaking to his lawyer Emil Bove - how will he cross examine Hope Hicks?

Justice Merchan: Please bring the witness out. Ms. Hicks, I remind you you are still under oath. Let's

get the jury, please.
[Jury entering]

Prosecutor: Did you witness a call between Mr. Trump and Mr. Cohen about this?

Hicks: After Ohio we flew to Hershey PA and we were getting into car. I heard Mr. Trump, there is nothing memorable about the call

Prosecutor: Where did you start the day?
Hicks: Maine

Prosecutor: The story about Karen McDougal, it quoted you - can you read it?

Hicks: "We have no knowledge of any of this... untrue."
Prosecutor: Did Mr. Trump tell you to say that?

Hicks: That was the consensus.
Prosecutor: By Mr. Trump?
Hicks: No romantic affair

Prosecutor: I'm going to show up your grand jury testimony

Hicks: As I sit here now I don't have a strong memory of him telling me we have no knowledge. These were hectic conversations.
Prosecutor: It says, "Mr. Davidson also represented Stephanie Clifford"

Prosecutor: Did you text with Mr. Cohen about this?
Hicks: Yes. Nov 4-5, 2016. Michael asked, Any news?? He wrote, "I don't see it getting much play." (Laughs) A little irony there.
Prosecutor: Then what?

Hicks: Michael said, it's Getting little to no traction.

Prosecutor: Mr. Cohen wrote he had a statement from Storm- what did you take that to mean?

Hicks: I didn't know and didn't know. I just wanted to blow past it and keep going. I asked for David Pecker's number, Mr. Trump wanted to speak to him

Hicks: Mr. Trump was concerned how his wife would see it. He asked me to make sure the newspapers weren't delivered to their residence the next morning

Prosecutor: When did you start working in the White House?

Hicks: Jan 20, 2027. I left between 2018 and 2020

Prosecutor: Where did you work from?

Hicks: Just outside the Oval. There were two desks, and a vestibule with a mini fridge and a coffee machine.
Prosecutor: Who was in the second desk next to you?
Hicks: Madeleine Westerhout.

Prosecutor: Were you aware Karen McDougal sued AMI to be released from her non-disclosure agreement?
Hicks: I've recently been refreshed.
Prosecutor: These text messages between you and Madeleine Westerhout, did your lawyer produce them under subpoena?
A: Yes

Prosecutor: When the Stormy Daniels story resurfaced, what next?
Hicks: President Trump told me Michael had paid about a false allegation, with him own money.
Prosecutor: What that consistent with what you

knew of Michael Cohen?

Hicks: No. He was not charitable

Prosecutor: No further questions.

Cross

Trump's lawyer Emil Bove: The Trump Organization created the communications position for you?

Hicks: Yes [seems to start crying]

Justice Merchan: Ms. Hicks do you need a break? [Seems so] Jurors, please step out

They're back [in interim, some views on X for Subscribers here]
Trump is conferring with both Bove and Blanche. Then

Hicks: Sorry about that.

Bove: You called it a family business

Hicks: Yes

Trump's lawyer Bove: You said Mr. Trump's relationship with Rhona Graff was respectful, yes?

Hicks: I really respected Rhona.
Bove: Then for the campaign, in 2015-16, Mr. Cohen wasn't part of the campaign, right?

Hicks: He would try to insert himself

Trump's lawyer Bove: Mr. Cohen was supposed to focus on Mr. Trump's business credentials - as a surrogate, yes?
Hicks: Yes.

Bove: He went rogue at times?

Hicks: He did. He liked to call himself a fixer - only because he first broke it (laughs)

Trump's lawyer Bove: President Trump's calls with Mr. Pecker didn't stick out, because he often spoke with the press?

Hicks: Right. He does a good job maintaining relationships with the media even if are negative on him.

Bove: Campaigns promote themselves?
Yes.

Trump's lawyer Bove: Campaigns do negative social media too, right?

Hicks: I've only been on one campaign, and it was a great one.
Bove: Did you travel with a laptop, send many messages?
Hicks: Yes.
Bove: There were constant inquiries about negative stories?
Yes.

Trump's lawyer Bove: Getting together to discuss coverage wasn't strange, was it?

Hicks: It wasn't.
Bove: There was the leak of President Trumps tax ingo - you also met about that?
Hicks: Yes

Bove: On Oct 8, he was worried.
Hicks: Yes, how it'd been seen at home

Trump's lawyer Bove: You've met Mrs. Trump, right?
Hicks: Yes. President Trump really respects her. She doesn't weigh in much, but when she does, he really listens.

Trump's lawyer Bove: In 2017, you didn't have anything to do with the business records of the Trump Organization 200 miles away, did you?
Hicks: No I didn't.

Bove: No further questions.

Prosecutor: I have nothing.

Justice Merchan: Please approach.

Then:
Justice Merchan: Jurors, we're going to call it a week. Do not read the news.
[Jurors and some others leave]
Justice Merchan: We can continue with the

Sandoval hearing.

Trump's lawyer Blanche: He shouldn't be cross examined about your contempt findings

Prosecutor: The Court of Appeals has said that contempt findings can be heard

Justice Merchan: They won't be here. Adjourned.

Hope

The Trump hotels gave me my break
Whatever came after I shouldn't be here
First the grand jury then this big room
It makes me want to cry
I'm sorry

I gave the prosecution that Cohen was a cheapskate
Then finish by praising the Boss
He's gagged so I don't know what he thinks
Yet